Let's Be Fit

Let's Be Fit

P. K. Hallinan

ideals children's books.

Nashville, Tennessee

ISBN-13: 978-0-8249-5528-1

Published by Ideals Children's Books
An imprint of Ideals Publications
A Guideposts Company
Nashville, Tennessee
www.idealsbooks.com

Color separations by Precision Color Graphics, Franklin, Wisconsin
Printed and bound in the United States of America

 Library of Congress Cataloging-in-Publication Data

Hallinan, P. K.
  Let's be fit! / by P.K. Hallinan.
     p. cm.
  ISBN 978-0-8249-5528-1 (alk. paper)
 1. Physical fitness--Juvenile literature. 2. Exercise--Juvenile
literature. I. Title.

 RA781.H337 2007
 613.7--dc22

2007008076

Designed by Georgina Chidlow-Rucker

10 9 8 7 6 5 4 3 2

This book is for

VALERIE

◆ ◆ ◆

From

mama

I like to be fit,
And I hope you agree

That being in shape
Is a great way to be!

It helps me with tasks—
I feel so much stronger.

It helps me in games—
I'm strong so much longer!

There's really no doubt that
I *think* better too,
For fitness assists me
In *all* that I do!

I watch what I eat—that's the place to begin.
I need to take heed of the food I take in.

So I sit down to eat a good balanced meal—
Lots of fresh greens and fruit are ideal.

I try to cut back
On sugary sweets,
For it's true what they say:
"You are what you eat."

Yes, getting in shape
Is a great thing to do.
And I have to stay active
And exercise too!

I try to do push-ups
And sit-ups each day.

I bend and I stretch
In a leisurely way.

I run just for fun
On the track at our school.

And I swim like a minnow
At our neighborhood pool.

But there's nothing quite like

A hill-and-dale hike!

Yes, fitness requires a change in the way
I look at the choices I make every day.
So, I'll scramble for chances to play out-of-doors!

I'll pour into chores like never before!

I'll drink lots of water
And get plenty of rest.

I'll tone up my body
Till I'm feeling my best.

And I'll strengthen my spirit
By keeping in mind
I'm wonderfully made,
And I'm one of a kind.

Yes, I'll run the good race—I won't falter or quit.

I'll just do what it takes . . .

To be physically fit.